LISTIFY

LISTIFY

LIST AND JOURNAL YOUR WAY TO BALANCE, SELF-DISCOVERY, AND SELF-CARE

MARINA GREENWAY

Mango Publishing
Coral Gables

Copyright © 2019 by Marina Greenway

Published by Mango Publishing Group, a division of Mango Media Inc.

Cover and Layout Design: Jermaine Lau

For permission requests, please contact the publisher at:

Mango Publishing Group
2850 Douglas Road, 2nd Floor
Coral Gables, FL 33134 USA
info@mango.bz

For special orders, quantity sales, course adoptions and corporate sales, please email the publisher at sales@mango.bz. For trade and wholesale sales, please contact Ingram Publisher Services at customer.service@ingramcontent.com or +1.800.509.4887.

Listify: List and Journal Your Way to Balance, Self-Discovery, and Self-Care

Library of Congress Cataloging
ISBN:(p) 978-1-64250-102-5 (e) 978-1-64250-103-2

Library of Congress Control Number: 2019938548

BISAC category code: OCC010000, BODY, MIND & SPIRIT / Mindfulness & Meditation

Printed in the United States of America

For Lola

Table of Contents

Introduction

This book will help you uncover the things your mind has been hiding. The stray tasks, the fun ideas, the meaningful memories. You will discover things about yourself you've never really thought about—like what activities drain you and which ones center you, your perfect day, your hidden aspirations, and more.

Who will help you discover all of this? You. The answers are all within. This friendly companion will simply guide you along the journey. But the benefit of this book is most powerful when you *return* to it. Having a bad day? You already have a list of all the movies that will make you smile and people you can call. Feeling drained? Just take a look at your list of all the activities that ground you, or re-explore your proudest accomplishments.

In this book, you will listify your way to peace and form a closer bond with yourself. The most ignored person in your life is often—yes—*you*. This book will help you reignite that self-love fire. With the lists and prompts in this book, you will become more mindful as you self-explore those unique, quirky things about yourself and the world around you.

Consider listifying and journaling as exercises in self-care. You deserve to chronicle all the beautiful aspects of your life. So, every day, put pen to paper and list or journal to a deeper connection with the most important person in your life—*you*.

Happy Listifying,

MARINA

PART 1

Gratitude

"Gratitude is where every positive attitude starts."

—Michael Hyatt and Daniel Harkavy

Ways I Can Show Gratitude to Myself and Others

It's important to show others we appreciate and care about them, but it's equally important to acknowledge ourselves and all we do. List the ways you can do so, and challenge yourself to do one from each list every day.

Myself   Others

_____   _____
_____   _____
_____   _____
_____   _____
_____   _____
_____   _____
_____   _____
_____   _____
_____   _____
_____   _____
_____   _____
_____   _____
_____   _____
_____   _____
_____   _____
_____   _____

Difficult Challenges That I Pushed Through (and What I Learned)

You have been through a lot. Pushed yourself, faced difficult situations, overcome challenges—all of it. List those moments and look back every now and then to acknowledge your journey and appreciate how far you've come.

"The greatest oak was once a little nut, who held its ground."

—UNKNOWN

Lately, I've Been Feeling...

Your state of mind changes over time and through the seasons. Record how you are feeling right now. What is going through your mind? Are you responding emotionally to something that has happened earlier in the week? Are you anticipating your day in a positive or negative way? What does your general state of being feel like? Do this every so often to chronicle your journey.

_____

_____

_____

_____

_____

_____

_____

_____

_____

_____

_____

_____

_____

_____

_____

_____

_____

People and Things I'm Grateful For

In addition to the wonderful people in your life, make room to be grateful for the other special things as well. The talents you were gifted with, your home that gives shelter and comfort, a text from your best friend. There are things that we unconsciously appreciate each day. Wrack your brain and list as many as you can think of. By the way, make sure *you* are on your list too.

_____

_____

_____

_____

_____

_____

_____

_____

_____

_____

_____

_____

_____

_____

_____

_____

_____

_____

_____

_____

The Memories I Will Always Cherish

Imagine someone turned on the highlight reel of your life. What would they see? What are the striking, vivid memories that shine the brightest in your life? What emotions are associated with them? Is there any common link between these memories?

_____

_____

_____

_____

_____

_____

_____

_____

_____

_____

_____

_____

_____

_____

_____

_____

_____

_____

_____

_____

_____

_____

Things That Always Make Me Smile

Whether it be comedians, jokes, memes, YouTube videos, or friends, list the things that always make you smile inside the smiley faces. Once you have this list, you can turn to it on the days when you are down.

I Would Describe My Personality and Sense of Humor As...

It's funny how sometimes people see us differently than we see ourselves. Explore how you define yourself, then share it with a friend to see if their description is different.

_____
_____
_____
_____
_____
_____
_____
_____
_____
_____
_____
_____
_____
_____
_____
_____
_____
_____
_____
_____
_____
_____

Today, I Will Take the Time to Appreciate...

List the things in your daily life that you want to give attention to and appreciate. A flower or tree you always pass on your way to work? The sound of silence? A friend's talent? The way the sky looks at sunset? It could be anything that you don't regularly acknowledge.

I Will Always Remember When ____ Said ____

Words are powerful. We've all had those times when people's words made a strong impression on us and changed us in ways we didn't expect. Whether it was a stranger giving a speech, someone who gave you advice, your grandmother telling you something about yourself, something you overheard in the hallway, or anything else under the sun, journal about the times when someone's words made a lasting impression.

_____
_____
_____
_____
_____
_____
_____
_____
_____
_____
_____
_____
_____
_____
_____
_____
_____
_____
_____
_____
_____
_____

Books, Movies, and Games That Give Me Comfort

We all have our favorites. Once you list yours, you will have something to come back to when you need some comforting TLC.

_____

_____

_____

_____

_____

_____

_____

_____

_____

_____

_____

_____

_____

_____

_____

_____

_____

_____

_____

_____

_____

_____

Acts of Kindness I've Seen Lately

There are acts of kindness around us every day, no matter how small. Did you see someone open the door for someone else behind them instead of pretending to not see them? Did a driver show courtesy to you or someone else? Start noticing all the acts of kindness around you (do some yourself too!), and the world will grow much brighter.

"The smallest act of kindness
is worth more than the
grandest intention."

—Oscar Wilde

People I Can Call Whenever I Need Them

Who are the people that are always there for you? List them and you'll have a resource handy whenever you have an internal emergency!

_____

_____

_____

_____

_____

_____

_____

_____

_____

_____

_____

_____

_____

_____

_____

_____

_____

_____

_____

_____

_____

Who can you call?

People Who I Will Always Be There For

Who are the people *you* are always there for? Gratitude and friendship go both ways—let these people know they can count on you.

_____

_____

_____

_____

_____

_____

_____

_____

_____

_____

_____

_____

_____

_____

_____

_____

_____

_____

_____

_____

Five Nice Things That Happened Today

It's easy to go through your day and see what's not going well. The next time you're feeling down, flip here and write down five things that made today a better day.

1. _____
2. _____
3. _____
4. _____
5. _____

1. _____
2. _____
3. _____
4. _____
5. _____

1. _____
2. _____
3. _____
4. _____
5. _____

1. _____
2. _____
3. _____
4. _____
5. _____

1. _____
2. _____
3. _____
4. _____
5. _____

1. _____
2. _____
3. _____
4. _____
5. _____

1. _____
2. _____
3. _____
4. _____
5. _____

1. _____
2. _____
3. _____
4. _____
5. _____

1. _____
2. _____
3. _____
4. _____
5. _____

1. _____
2. _____
3. _____
4. _____
5. _____

1. _____
2. _____
3. _____
4. _____
5. _____

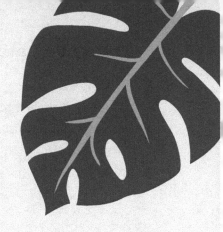

PART 2

Balance

"Nature does not hurry, yet everything is accomplished."

—Lao Tzu

Things I'd Rather Not Do, Thanks Very Much

Our time and energy are precious. Spend it only on the things that are important to *you*. Confucius once said: "To go beyond is as wrong as to fall short." Don't let unwanted or unneeded tasks rule your life. If you need an idea of how to start this list, think of the things you were too polite to say no to, and go from there.

_____

_____

_____

_____

_____

_____

_____

_____

_____

_____

_____

_____

_____

_____

_____

_____

"These mountains that you are carrying, you were only supposed to climb."

—NAJWA ZEBIAN

A Perfect Day Would Go Like This...

We know that things can't *always* go exactly the way we want. But life is too short not to *try*. Describe how a perfect day would go if you had something to say about it. (And you do!)

_____

_____

_____

_____

_____

_____

_____

_____

_____

_____

_____

_____

_____

_____

_____

_____

_____

_____

_____

_____

_____

_____

_____

"This a wonderful day. I've
never seen this one before."

—Maya Angelou

These Activities (or Relaxivities) Help Me Center Myself

Whether it be journaling, yoga, or cuddling with your pet, list those relaxing activities that bring back your balance and sense of self.

_____

_____

_____

_____

_____

_____

_____

_____

_____

_____

_____

_____

_____

_____

_____

_____

_____

_____

_____

_____

_____

_____

_____

If I Could Only Own Five Items for the Rest of My Life...

What possessions would you keep if you were only allowed five? Aside from necessities like toothpaste, of course. Doodle them here.

People Dis-pleasers

You can list toxic people, habits, or environments that you'd rather avoid here. Habits can include gossiping, negative self-talk, or anything that is harmful to your mental state or harmful to others.

The Joy of Jotting It Down

Sometimes our brains simply can't hold onto all the things we're supposed to remember, like that payment confirmation number you pretended to be ready for, the ingredients you need for tonight's recipe, or the book recommendation your friend gave you. Use these pages to jot down all the random ideas, fun facts, to-dos, or other notes that don't really belong anywhere. They now have a home right here! Think of this as a lovely "brain dump" landfill.

Nearby Parks and Attractions to Explore

We all know how it goes—we are on our way somewhere, busy doing something, or simply scrolling through our social media feed and looking at all the fun other people are having and think, "Hey, I wanna do that!" Jot down all the cool parts of town, lovely-looking parks, museums, zoos, or butterfly gardens you want explore around your area.

Letting Go = More Room for Joy

What baggage haven't you left behind yet? Is it an old friend you regret losing touch with? Hurt from an old flame? Whatever it is, it's holding you back from moving forward. Write down a regret in each bird and let it go.

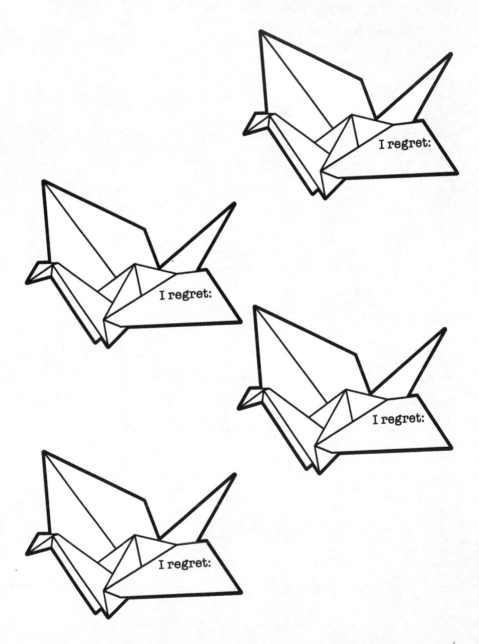

Upcoming Events or Concerts to Attend

Everyone needs something to look forward to! What festivals or musical artists are heading your way? Check out websites like Eventbrite and festivals.com, as well as your local news outlets to stay on top of what's happening near you!

My Favorite Places, Real and Fictional

List the places you'd love to get the chance to see plus the ones you already have been to, whether in body or mind. Speaking of which...did you know the Shire and Gringotts are real places you can visit?

_____

_____

_____

_____

_____

_____

_____

_____

_____

_____

_____

_____

_____

_____

_____

_____

_____

_____

_____

_____

_____

_____

_____

"Relax. Nothing is under control."

—ADI DA

Turn That Negative Self-Talk Around

We let too many things pass in our internal dialogue that we would never say to anyone else. Would you tell your best friend, "Oh *wow*, you so look bloated right now," "You're such an idiot," or "You aren't talented or smart enough to do that"? You *know* that you've said these to yourself at some point. It's time to end negative self-talk once and for all. List the negative things you say to yourself regularly. You can also list them as they occur. Then, combat it with a positive solution or compliment (or both). I've added some examples to get you started.

Instead of this...	This!
I look so tired right now	I will go to sleep earlier tonight
My handwriting is terrible	I write beautiful poems
I'm not smart enough	I love learning new things

Instead of this...   **This!**

_____   _____
_____   _____
_____   _____
_____   _____
_____   _____
_____   _____
_____   _____
_____   _____
_____   _____
_____   _____
_____   _____
_____   _____
_____   _____
_____   _____
_____   _____
_____   _____
_____   _____
_____   _____
_____   _____
_____   _____
_____   _____
_____   _____
_____   _____
_____   _____
_____   _____
_____   _____

Instead of this... This!

I Will Treat Myself To...

Sometimes a little TLC is all we need when times gets tough or we're just annoyed with life in general. Be generous and treat yourself to any of the items or outings on this list when you need it.

Treat yourself!

_____   _____
_____   _____
_____   _____
_____   _____
_____   _____
_____   _____
_____   _____
_____   _____
_____   _____
_____   _____
_____   _____
_____   _____
_____   _____
_____   _____
_____   _____
_____   _____

"*I am always doing that which I cannot do, in order that I may learn how to do it.*"

—PABLO PICASSO

Best Advice I've Ever Gotten

It's always easy to give advice, but it's much harder to apply advice given to us. But sometimes, there are words of wisdom that knock us sideways in how true and impactful they turn out to be. What great advice have you gotten? Who gave it to you?

_____
_____
_____
_____
_____
_____
_____
_____
_____
_____
_____
_____
_____
_____
_____
_____
_____
_____

Dream Vacation Spots

What destinations come to mind when you think of the word "vacation"? Here are some lovely spots to spark your imagination: Chile, Paris, Bali, Joshua Tree National Park, Niagara Falls, keep going!

In My Free Time...

List all the activities you enjoy doing in your free time. Also, are there things you *wish* you did in your free time? Make sure you star those entries.

_____

_____

_____

_____

_____

_____

_____

_____

_____

_____

_____

_____

_____

_____

_____

_____

_____

_____

_____

_____

It's All You

What do *you* need to keep track of? Create your own list here of whatever you want! New pet names, recipes to try, daily writing goals: use this page to keep track of 'em!

_____

_____

_____

_____

_____

_____

_____

_____

_____

_____

_____

_____

_____

_____

_____

_____

_____

_____

_____

_____

_____

_____

_____

_____

Things I Want to Accomplish Every Day

Do you want to have an hour of "me time" every day, play catch with your dog, or eat home-cooked meals? No desire is too big or small. What do you want to accomplish every single day?

_____

_____

_____

_____

_____

_____

_____

_____

_____

_____

_____

_____

_____

_____

_____

_____

_____

_____

_____

_____

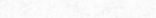

PART 3

Kindness

"The fragrance always stays in the hand that gives the rose."

—Hada Bejar

People I Want to Get to Know Better

Here's an idea: next to the person's name, write the first step you can take to make it happen. Perhaps a phone call, coffee date, or outing at the dog park? No one can resist the dog park.

Who?

Ideas to Make It Happen

_____ _____
_____ _____
_____ _____
_____ _____
_____ _____
_____ _____
_____ _____
_____ _____
_____ _____
_____ _____
_____ _____
_____ _____
_____ _____
_____ _____
_____ _____
_____ _____

Ways I Can Be Kind to Strangers

Sometimes we don't recognize opportunities for kindness because we don't make it a point to. It happens to the best of us. Brainstorm a list of simple things you can do to show kindness to others. Now you'll have a resource to get ideas from every day!

"Kindness makes a fellow feel good whether it's being done to him or by him."

—FRANK A. CLARK

In a Perfect World

There is a great deal of literature out there on what utopia would look like and if it could ever even be possible (read a few books and see what you think). But if it *were* possible, what would your ideal world look like? Would crowded cities be banned because everyone now lives in an idyllic shire? What sort of economic system would we have? Would we go back to bartering? Trading poetry for food? Explore.

_____
_____
_____
_____
_____
_____
_____
_____
_____
_____
_____
_____
_____
_____
_____
_____
_____
_____

The Only One in the World

It's a relief we are all different! Why do some people think it's a bad thing? If we all had the same background, culture, upbringing, and interests—oh dear. The world would be *so* dull, and we'd still be living in the dark ages. For those days you need reminding (and we all do sometimes), list all the ways you are unique here.

"To love oneself is the beginning of a lifelong romance."

—Oscar Wilde

Heartful Meditation

Many studies have shown the benefits of meditation. It can lower blood pressure, provide more restful sleep, and lessen anxiety, among many other near-magical benefits. What are you waiting for? Try it now. There are many wonderful videos and apps out there (*Headspace* and *Simple Habit* are my favorites). But first, set an intention. Do you want recognize it as special "me time"? Is your intention for stress relief? A better attention span? Whatever your intention, once you complete the meditation, note your impressions here. What was your intention? Was it difficult to relax? What thoughts crossed your mind? How do you feel now?

_____

_____

_____

_____

_____

_____

_____

_____

_____

_____

_____

_____

_____

_____

_____

_____

I Will Include ___ in My Thoughts and Prayers

Sometimes, it's a challenge to remember everyone's name on your mental prayer list. List all of the people and causes you don't want to forget to remember!

_____

_____

_____

_____

_____

_____

_____

_____

_____

_____

_____

_____

_____

_____

_____

_____

_____

_____

_____

_____

_____

_____

Ways I Can Give Back to My Community

We all have causes we are passionate about. Are you inspired to comfort women in difficult times? Seek out a women's shelter to see how you can help. Are you passionate about education? Contact local schools to find opportunities for volunteering. Find ways to give back and support your community, and list them here. Try to check them off regularly throughout the year. Giving back is the greatest way to show kindness to the world.

"Give without remembering and always receive without forgetting."

—Unknown

Organizations to Donate to / Volunteer For

If you can't afford regular donations to your charity or nonprofit of choice, give the gift of your time a few times a month (or as often as you can). List your preferred organizations here.

_____

_____

_____

_____

_____

_____

_____

_____

_____

_____

_____

_____

_____

_____

_____

_____

_____

_____

_____

_____

"Great opportunities to help others seldom come, but small ones surround us every day."

—Sally Koch

Affirm **Your Life**

List affirmations or favorite quotes that empower you and (most importantly) scare you. Make them daring, aspirational, dream-fueled ones that will push your life in the right direction. Make this fun by doodling some in a special font and emphasizing certain words. Spice them up and make them your own.

"As I say yes to life, life says yes to me."

—LOUISE HAY

People and Actions I Have Forgiven

It's been said one shouldn't keep score of the tough moments, but it's good to remember how far you've come and how deeply you have forgiven. That way, the next time someone in your life needs forgiveness (and they will)...well, you've done it before and here is the proof.

_____

_____

_____

_____

_____

_____

_____

_____

_____

_____

_____

_____

_____

_____

_____

_____

_____

_____

_____

_____

"Forgive others, not because they deserve forgiveness, but because you deserve peace."

—JONATHAN HUIE

People I Choose to Forgive Today

If you are still in the process of forgiveness, writing it down helps make it so. Try it now. Write: I forgive ___. Feel the release.

I forgive...

_____

_____

_____

_____

_____

_____

_____

_____

_____

_____

_____

_____

_____

_____

_____

_____

_____

_____

_____

_____

_____

_____

_____

"Forgiveness is the fragrance
that the violet sheds on the
heel that has crushed it."

—Mark Twain

Compliments I Can to Give Others (and Myself)

Helping others feel great will in turn make *you* feel great. Acknowledge someone's hard work, compliment something about their appearance, or simply let them know you think they are amazing. There is joy in lifting others up. Don't forget to do the same to yourself! You deserve just as much praise and appreciation.

_____

_____

_____

_____

_____

_____

_____

_____

_____

_____

_____

_____

_____

_____

_____

_____

_____

_____

"You are very powerful,
provided you know how
powerful you are."

—YOGI BHAJAN

How I Can Support a Friend or Family Member Who Is Struggling

If you need ideas, think of what brings you comfort in troubling times. Does it help to simply have someone *listen*? Do you prefer your loved ones to tell you the honest truth, instead of what you want to hear? Use your judgment. If someone you know is in a serious situation, don't look away. Here are some resources to help.

Resources in Crisis

National Suicide Prevention Lifeline: **1-800-273-8255**

National Domestic Violence Hotline: **1-800-799-7233**

Lifeline Crisis Chat: **www.contact-usa.org/chat. html**

Family Violence Helpline: **1-800-996-6228**

The Trevor Project: **1-866-488-7386**

Veterans Crisis Line: **1-800-273-8255 or www.veteranscrisisline.net**

Planned Parenthood Hotline: **1-800-230-7526**

My Favorite Things about My Favorite People

There are very few friends you would ditch Netflix in bed for. Who are you favorite people? What are those amazing things you just love about them?

_____

_____

_____

_____

_____

_____

_____

_____

_____

_____

_____

_____

_____

_____

_____

_____

_____

_____

_____

_____

_____

"What lies behind us and what lies before us are tiny matters compared to what lies within us."

—RALPH WALDO EMERSON

My Ideal Self-Care Routine

Check off each day you complete your routine this month!

My ideal routine...

_____

_____

_____

_____

_____

_____

_____

Month:

SUNDAY	MONDAY	TUESDAY	WEDNESDAY	THURSDAY	FRIDAY	SATURDAY

Month:

SUNDAY	MONDAY	TUESDAY	WEDNESDAY	THURSDAY	FRIDAY	SATURDAY

_____

_____

_____

_____

_____

_____

_____

_____

_____

_____

Jokes That Make Me Smile

That's easy! *All* bad dad jokes, right? What does a pepper do when it's angry? It gets jalapeño face!

Love and Friendship

It is too often that we don't recognize what is important to us in friends or partners. What does a healthy romantic relationship look like to you? What about a healthy friendship? What qualities does an ideal friend and/or romantic partner have?

_____

_____

_____

_____

_____

_____

_____

_____

_____

_____

_____

_____

_____

_____

_____

_____

_____

_____

_____

PART 4

Joy

"A flower blossoms for its own joy."

—Oscar Wilde

People That Encourage Me

Whether they're notable figures who have achieved something amazing or the people in your life who have always been there for you, list all of the people who have encouraged you. If you let them know how much they've inspired you, you might in turn give *them* encouragement.

Music That Always Cheers Me Up

What songs, artists, or bands always bring a smile to your face?
Put on your favorite playlist and write them here!

_____

_____

_____

_____

_____

_____

_____

_____

_____

_____

_____

_____

_____

_____

_____

_____

_____

_____

_____

Favorite Animal Encounters

Seeing cute dogs on the sidewalk or at the park is one of the joys of life. Have you seen a cat on a leash recently too? Cuddled with a bunny at the pet store? Capturing these memories is guaranteed to bring you joy!

Creatures (Real or Fictional) I Love

From Fawkes to Smaug, Buckbeak to Babe, who are your favorite pwecious creatures? List or doodle them below.

My Favorite Scents

During Potions class in Harry Potter, the students are asked to brew a love potion. Once the potions are ready, though they all have the same ingredients, they all smell differently (depending on the person who is smelling it!). Hermione's smelled like freshly mown grass, new parchment, and spearmint toothpaste...her favorite scents. What might yours smell like?

Explore Your Memories Through Your Nose...

It has happened to all of us: out of the blue, we catch a whiff of something that throws us back into some childhood memory, reminds us of a person we used to know, or makes us feel a certain way. Think back to some of the times this has happened and the strongest feelings you've had. They might reveal something important.

Quotes That Inspire Me

There's a surplus of witty or inspiring words of wisdom out there—yet, once in a while, we see a few that truly stick with us. Capture those here for much-needed inspiration when you get sidetracked and out of focus.

_____
_____
_____
_____
_____
_____
_____
_____
_____
_____
_____

_____
_____
_____
_____
_____
_____
_____
_____
_____
_____

"People lose their way when they lose their why."

—GAIL HYATT

Movie Marathon Films and Snacks

What new or old movies have you been dying to see? Arm yourself with mind-blowing entertainment and the perfect snacks for those much-needed movie marathon nights!

Snacks	Movies
_____	_____
_____	_____
_____	_____
_____	_____
_____	_____
_____	_____
_____	_____
_____	_____
_____	_____
_____	_____
_____	_____
_____	_____
_____	_____
_____	_____
_____	_____
_____	_____
_____	_____
_____	_____

Favorite Fun Facts about Myself

List the facts people might not know about you. Do you have secrets talents? Interesting hobbies?

_____

_____

_____

_____

_____

_____

_____

_____

_____

_____

_____

_____

_____

_____

_____

_____

_____

_____

_____

_____

_____

_____

_____

"*Always remember that you are absolutely unique. Just like everyone else.*"

—Margaret Mead

My Little Dream Journal...

Some people have recurring dreams, as well as strange dreams that come and go without explanation. Some remember every dream they've had, some only a rare few. Note down some of your memorable dreams and look for any common themes. Perhaps you'll discover something interesting.

_____

_____

_____

_____

_____

_____

_____

_____

_____

_____

_____

_____

_____

_____

_____

_____

_____

_____

_____

_____

_____

_____

_____

Witty Things I've Said That I'm Proud Of

Don't be shy—we've all got those cool one-liners and awesome quips that we're proud of (even if you only thought of them after the conversation was over). Note them all down here and you'll always have something to make you smile.

My All-Time Proudest Accomplishments

From getting awards to getting over everyday hurdles (like managing to keep your cool with that rude person on the bus—everyone's going through something), list your proudest accomplishments here. Go wide and deep—you have achieved more than you think!

Things I Will Miss When I'm Gone

One day, the inevitable will happen. What will you miss from this world? The way the stars look reflected on the water...the sound of the forest? The smell of baking bread...the taste?

_____

_____

_____

_____

_____

_____

_____

_____

_____

_____

_____

_____

_____

_____

_____

_____

_____

_____

_____

_____

If I Had Magical Powers...

We are never too old to admit we wish we had magical powers. Admit it! What would yours be? What would you do with it? What do you think your non-magical superpower is right now?

_____

_____

_____

_____

_____

_____

_____

_____

_____

_____

_____

_____

_____

_____

_____

_____

_____

_____

_____

_____

_____

"*It always seems impossible until it's done.*"

—Nelson Mandela

The Joy of Tic-Tac-Toe

Sometimes the simple games are the most fun. Challenge a friend to the classic childhood game of tic-tac-toe, and treat the winner to an ice cream or other delicacy you enjoyed when you were younger.

We All Have a Dream

Write about a dream of yours and the "why" behind it. When did it begin? Why is it so important to you? What is holding you back right now?

"A year from now you will wish you had started today."

—KAREN LAMB

My Favorite Books

Books let us live multiple lives without ever leaving our couches!
What books or short stories are your all-time favorites?

_____

_____

_____

_____

_____

_____

_____

_____

_____

_____

_____

_____

_____

_____

_____

_____

_____

_____

_____

_____

My Favorite Movies

From guilty pleasures to Oscar-winners, we've all got our special favorites. Which ones are yours?

About the Author

Marina Greenway is a lifelong list and literature lover from the tropical shire of Miami. She enjoys journaling and putting together lists, bullet journals, and other fun organizing systems. This hobby inspired her to pen the Listify series for all who also enjoy chronicling their lives on paper. Inspired by her studies in English literature, Marina is a firm believer in reading and writing as means of creative release, fun, and self-care. She can be found on Instagram at @_MarinaGreenway_ where she shares writing, listing, and organizing inspiration, book reviews, and adorable pictures of her Yorkie, Lola.

Marina Greenway